LET YOUR LIGHT

*Short Stories of Men and Women
Who Shone Christ*

M. MORKOS

ST MARY & MOSES ABBEY PRESS

Let Your Light: Short Stories of Men and Women Who Shone Christ

By M. Morkos

Designed & Published by:
St. Mary & St. Moses Abbey Press
101 S Vista Dr, Sandia, TX 78383
stmabbeypress.com

Cover illustration and design by Sandra Latif.

Contents

✠

O the true Light who shines upon every man who comes into the world, You came into the world by Your love for mankind.... As the daylight shines on us, let the luminous senses and the bright thoughts shine in us...

Troparia of the First Hour,

from the Coptic Book of Hours

Preface

Surely we all judge books by their covers, despite the old adage warning us not to. Regardless of the packaging, a truly good book (or movie, or article) nudges me to my knees to know God better—or at the very least move from point A to point B. The hope is that the book in your hands does the same, not because it is "good," but because it shares the stories of individuals who in some form encountered Jesus, the Source and Giver of all truth and light.

Each short story shares what a particular individual, or surrounding characters, may have thought, said, and done in a brief snapshot of his/her life. Not all details are supplied right away, so we may slowly discover and meet the person. Some stories are well-known, while perhaps one or two will be new. Regardless, each account is meant to place us directly inside the individual's life so that by the book's end, we continue (or begin) to encounter the Word of God as it really is: "living and active" as St. Paul declares in the epistle to the Hebrews.

With the background that hagiography is a difficult genre for academic study, attention was given to historical accuracy whenever possible. Content was gathered from Scripture and sources based on Orthodox tradition. If a particular person was written about in more than one gospel, I attempted to include details from all the accounts. Descriptions I supplied were informed by modern scholars' knowledge of the cultural, geo-political, and religious norms of the time. At the end of each account, I briefly shared where imagination filled the spaces that history has left blank.

The individuals of these stories come from varying backgrounds and temperaments, and thus their experiences of Jesus must have differed. It stands to reason from direct evidence or informed deduction that each person whose story is written here could not remain the same after encountering Christ. In other words, Jesus completely changed their lives. I have imagined many times how impossible it must have been for any of them to afterwards keep their newfound light from others.

Despite all their and our differences, God *must* delight in each of us experiencing His grace and love if we so choose. I am inclined to think that God's family would not be quite the same if even one of us did not let our light—uniquely yours and uniquely mine—shine for all to see. May we always experience the True Light who gives light to every person, through these pages and in all things.

"You [insert your name here] are the light of the world. A city that is set on a hill cannot be hidden. Nor do they light a lamp and put it under a basket, but on a lampstand, and it gives light to all who are in the house. Let your light so shine before men, that they may see your good works and glorify your Father in heaven."[1]

---

1   Matthew 5:14–16.

Gold

Zavah. Zavah. Zavah.

She quickened her pace. The word lingered in her mind as though she was hearing the women in the marketplace whispering it. She knew no one was nearby glancing at her covertly, as she was accustomed to. In fact, the path was unusually quiet as a large crowd had just hurried past. Yet the word repeated itself over and over in her mind. Random onlookers used to say it audibly, but at this point she was a lost cause. It was as if some cruel pity forced people to shun her now in hushed secrecy rather than publicly.

Zavah! Zavah, zavah, zavah.

With each mental repetition of the word, she felt the usual pain climb up her face. It was the same pressure she experienced since the illness began, whenever strangers would stare at her and then turn away. The emotional pain used to be more difficult to bear than the bleeding itself, but both were now daily facts of life. They were a part of her, and nothing could change this reality. She had finally accepted it.

Dirty zavah!

Her tears were unusually bitter today. She wiped them quickly from her cheeks and hugged her shawl closer, walking faster. The tattered article was all that she had left of any monetary worth, the only thing that was allowed to touch her. By it she tried to remember the warmth of her mother's embrace, but many memories were fading. Shaking her head to rid herself of these futile thoughts, she shut her eyes tightly for a moment to push down the growing fear inside of her. Recently this anxiety had started to physically paralyze her. But today it could *not*. She had to keep walking towards the crowd. One last meal was all that the leftover grain would provide, so begging would soon be her dinner companion. The fear of starving had to be kept at bay for the moment.

Zahava, daughter!

She remembered much better days, especially her father's house full of servants. She was never then in want of either food or love, and the fleeting memories of that time warmed her now lonely days and cold nights. Images of her younger self quickly came to mind: first running, then skipping, then running again ahead of her mother and father. They were on their way to the temple for a feast, and the pair were walking behind her in quiet contentment.

Her father, wanting to know if she was tired or hungry, from time to time would call out her name. Zahava never tired from hearing him say it, with the syllables always lingering in the wind. How strangely similar it sounded to *zavah*, her current identity.

She remembered how confident she was of God's love and generosity then as a young child. Did not Moses teach them that the Lord was compassionate and merciful? She was even to be engaged, and then— *zavah*. The illness came, and for a long time the family held onto any small hope that this doctor, then that one, could heal her. The treatments became longer, costlier. Her body became weaker and wracked with growing layers of pain. The family's monetary reserve slowly dwindled, and so did the flickering dream of one day being whole again.

She had run out of options and friendships, and eventually even the goodwill of her family. If this illness was lasting for so long, surely God must not be happy with her. That is what the people initially rumored about her, what her parents refused to believe for so long. Her father and mother stood by her at first. But after a decade of unanswered prayers, she could not blame them. The conclusion that she must be cursed, unloved, could not be easily refuted.

I will always be a zavah. She suddenly broke into a run when this thought passed through her mind.

Despite her vision being blurred by tears, she knew she was quickly approaching the swarm of people. She had nothing to lose at this point. No dignity was left in her bosom. She would go straight through it. She would go straight through the crowd. The people would be horrified, yes. But it had to be done. She had quite literally nothing, and no one, else.

Earlier that day she had overheard several townspeople saying He was on the way to a ruler's house to heal a young girl. *Am I not also a young woman*, she thought to herself, *once proudly able to speak of the high position of my own family?* Didn't they say He had healed a demon-possessed man? Could a bleeding woman be much worse?

At this point she started moving into the crowd, and the shocked expressions began to appear as people recognized her. She shuddered as she thought, *They will have to go through the purification rituals.* People began to move away from her, and comments of disgust became audible. *Perhaps*, she told herself, *He could take away some of the pain. Not all of it, but perhaps my family would accept me again, even as a zavah*. She was now moving directly towards the tall figure amidst His disciples. This part of the crowd had not noticed her, and everyone was still conversing loudly as they walked. It became noisier the closer she approached Him. She had to focus to think above the clatter—*Just His hem*, she thought, *I could be better by just touching His clothes.*

She had lunged forward and thought she lost consciousness in doing so; all was so completely quiet. Yet here she was, standing and very much alert. She was just a few feet away from Jesus and saw that the crowd had come to a standstill. He seemed to have said something unusual to His followers, because they were looking incredulously at Him. One man scoffed as he said, "Master, the multitude is thronging You, and You say, 'Who touched me?'"

She froze. He knew! He knew someone defiled had touched His hem! She was waiting for the pain to climb up her face again, for the fear to paralyze her limbs. But at that moment she realized how *light* she felt—the bleeding had stopped! In fact, in the few moments since she touched His garment, the pain had also vanished, and she even felt *clean*. It was as though she were almost fully whole and complete.

She then heard Him respond in a low, authoritative voice to the man, "Somebody touched Me, for I perceived power going out from Me."

Trembling, she moved forward closer to Him, not daring to make eye contact. She fell to her hands and knees, with her lips just inches from the ground, as though she was talking directly to the earth.

"Master, I—I touched you. I am a *zavah*, a bleeding woman. For twelve years I have gotten worse and have lost—everything. I stopped hoping. Until I heard of You. I touched—I touched You to be better. And I was healed, immediately!"

There was an immediate murmuring amongst the crowd in response to this, with many scattered looks of doubt and a few nods of approval.

Jesus held out His hands to help her up. "Daughter." At this, she could not hide her surprise and instinctively raised her eyes to meet His. She saw in them strength, and comfort, and acceptance. He had said the word "daughter" so much like her father that He might as well have said her name, Zahava. He smiled at her astonishment. "Be of good cheer; your faith has made you well. Go in peace."

With this He turned to another person who had come quickly towards him, evidently needing His attention. Some of His disciples nodded to her farewell; they had seen similar looks of amazement many times before.

For several moments Zahava looked after Him and the accompanying crowd as they became smaller and smaller in the distance. A few minutes ago, before He spoke with her, she had felt physical newness. When Jesus had called her daughter, had *seen* her, when *He* had touched *her*—she knew that her internal pain was gone too, for good. She now felt completely full. She *was* loved, deeply. She *was* precious. Zahava felt, for the first time in a long while, exactly what her name meant: gold.

The accounts of this remarkable miracle are found in Matthew 9:20–22, Mark 5:25–34, and Luke 8:43–48. We do not know much about this woman, including her actual name. We do know that Jewish contact with blood was strictly forbidden as dictated by the book of Leviticus, so she very likely lived in religious and social isolation. We experience this woman's life-changing transformation through the above gospel passages.

Lavender

The sweet, nostalgic scent filled her nostrils and immediately brought a smile to her face. She opened her wearied eyes and scanned the fields next to the road on which the soldier forced her to march. There they were! Incredible! What a gift! Her heart pounded with joy, and she forcefully subdued the happiness that wanted to burst out of her. It was as if He wanted to say, "I met you that day for the first time, but we will meet again soon."

Her lips quivered as she was overwhelmed by heavenly love. She still did not think she deserved to know Him, even after all this time. She looked heavenward, and the sun beamed golden rays on her sallow face. Despite the ragged linen hanging loosely on her disfigured limbs, she felt enveloped by warmth. Her mind went back to the earlier days of constantly stumbling in pained loneliness.

Looking at the ground was always the safest way; safest for her bruised emotions and battered mind; safest for others so they would not have to make eye contact with her. She looked at the well-worn, and well-known, path. She knew in one, two, three-and-a-half steps she would be out of the shade of the silent marketplace, and the scent of lavender would overwhelm her on the sun-dripped road. The heat that the merchants and villagers escaped to enjoy their midday meals had now intensified. Yet she felt the usual coldness inside her. It was more than that—she felt *dry*. She scoffed at herself, at what she was about to do, and the irony of the situation. Why? Why couldn't she simply feel less *parched*? It was a deep emptiness difficult to put into words. Sighing with gloomy remorse, she knew that *this* one was not going to fill her. The five others did not. Why was she such a fool?

She never raised her head while walking this path, but at that moment in her agonized guilt and self-disgust, she inadvertently looked up. Someone must have forgotten a pitcher—no, it had moved! Could it really be a man? She froze in her steps, but it was too late. He had looked up and saw her approaching. She could not turn around now. She hesitated, then walked slowly, falteringly, trying to avoid His gaze. Who tried to draw water at this hour, besides her? Was this a cruel joke from one of the villagers? No, the one glimpse she had of His face showed Him to be very tired. He must have stopped for a drink. She looked up slightly and saw His dusty tunic. What! The Man was a Jew! What was He doing here, at our well, of all—

"Give me a drink."

She froze at the Man's words. He was now only a few paces away from her, and she looked up at Him, with a thousand questions and challenges immediately rising to her lips. He looked intently at her, as though He would repeat the command. Clearly, He was waiting for her response.

"How is it—" She faltered, trying to place into a single question the multitude of swirling thoughts and emotions inside of her. *How is it that I have come here so often*, she thought to herself, *and drank from this wretched well so many times, and yet... I feel more insignificant than the dust underneath my feet? How is it that the ground I stand on is more watered, more satiated than I?*

She wanted to say all of this to Him, although she was not sure why. But instead, she started again:

"How is it, that You, being a Jew, ask a drink from me, a Samaritan woman?"

She expected Him to simply take the waterpot and help Himself in response, or somehow know who she was and mock her. She was, after all, familiar with ridicule. Or, as she quietly hoped, perhaps He would simply leave her and look for a drink elsewhere. But to her surprise and dismay, He did not seem rushed at all to drink. In fact, it became clear that drinking water was not His objective at this moment at all. He was looking at her, to converse with her!

Before she knew it, they made a few exchanges. This unusual Man claimed He had special water. When she tried to respond, something buried deep inside of her came up with painful, raw vulnerability. She said with a faltering voice, "Sir, give me this water." She stopped to swallow the lump in her throat. "Give me this water that I may not—not thirst, nor come here to draw."

They talked again for several more moments, her thoughts whirling from what she was hearing. Did He just say He was the long-awaited *Messiah*?

Photini remembered running into the town after this meeting with Jesus, lavender wafting on the summer air. He had filled—should she rather say *quenched*?—her ever-present, inner thirst. Yet they had not drunk water the entire time! Indeed, she listened to His teachings with the rest of Samaria for two entire days afterward. How life-giving were His words! How sweet it was to share the good news with person after person, weeks and months and years after their meeting at Jacob's well. Since the Resurrection, she could not count the number of lives turned upside down as hers had done.

Photini knew then as she did now that she could not keep His teachings to herself. That is how she ended up here in Rome, but not without a cost. Many people dear to her were laying down their lives, one by one, for Him. Photini thought to herself, *how bittersweet it is to truly love and then let go!* But she knew the Truth in which she believed. Wasn't the Holy Spirit working daily—comforting, healing, converting?

No matter, then, that this was likely where she would spend her last days. Did not the guard say she would be thrown into a *well*? The paradox was not lost on her, and Photini laughed. *I must look like a madwoman!* she thought. Who would laugh on their way to certain death?

She could. She knew God was always with her and would forever satisfy her deepest needs. She had first met Him unwillingly at the well in Sychar many years ago, when she most acutely felt her life was aimless and pitifully empty. Now thousands of miles away, Photini was walking resolutely towards another well, with a devoted and overflowing heart.

And here again were lavender blooms! Without a single word or miracle, God was once more reassuring her of His sovereignty. This certainly seemed like an ending. But Photini knew that soon she would simply be meeting Him again.

Through Tradition we know that the Samaritan woman in John 4:4–42 eventually was baptized with the name Photini. St. Photini became a great evangelist and martyr during Emperor Nero's reign. She converted many to the faith, including her five sisters and Nero's own daughter. Her name comes from the Greek word for "bright" or "enlightened one."

Royal

"If I so much as catch the scent of any more bullying, you will most certainly see me again!"

The young ruffians hastily ran away at this final threat, kicking up clouds of dust behind them. The elegant woman who had spoken these words, having kept a severe demeanor while reproaching the children, now suddenly broke out into a radiant smile. The little boy who cowered near the wall, still trembling from this newest round of taunting, felt the softness of the stranger's kind eyes. Despite his young age, he instinctively knew she was from nobility. Besides, his mother had told him that only the very rich wore clothes of such lovely colors. The woman reached out to hold his hand and help him up, quietly dusting off his ragged clothes. He looked inquisitively at her, his innocent heart perceiving that she was more beautiful than other women.

"Where is your papa?" the woman asked the little boy.

"Dead, good lady."

Her face resumed its sternness, this time at the child's misfortunes.

"Where is your mama?" she asked in a quieter tone, dusting off his hair.

"Working."

"How many dates did they steal from you?"

"This much." He cupped his dirty hands together to show her. "That is all I could buy."

The woman gently took one of his hands in hers as she walked to the neighboring stall and spoke with the vendor.

"A basket, please," as she pointed to the dates. "And," she added quietly to the man, "please tell me if they ever bother him again. I want to know immediately."

"Yes, your excellency!"

The lady handed the boy a large basket of dates, and he looked at them with astonishment.

"Give this also to your mama when she comes home," and the lady slipped a bag of gold coins into the basket.

"This is—a lot to eat!" The boy's little mind did not bother with the bag of money, thinking only of how to eat all the dates in one sitting.

The lady laughed. "Is home close by?" she asked.

The boy nodded his disheveled head. The lady knelt down, looked him directly in the eyes, and said in a barely audible whisper as she pointed to the sky, "Do you know your Heavenly Father is a King, and He is always protecting you?"

The boy nodded again, his small muddied face lighting up a little. Just then, his growling stomach reminded him of the sweet fruit in his possession. After replicating a deep bow he once saw a merchant give to a well-dressed patron, the little boy quickly ran towards his home.

The lady straightened up again, smoothed out the front of her silk dress, and with her usual dignified posture started walking briskly towards her own home. She got there in no time, it seemed; her mind was busy with the same thoughts that were interrupted when she first saw the older boys intimidating her new little friend.

She started pacing in the courtyard and its gardens. There was no doubt in her mind where the truth lay. She had listened often to the Elder, reflected, and listened some more. She tried to pray constantly, vigorously, and intentionally. How her spirit was still fed by the memories of the Savior's apparitions that were allowed her!

Of course, not unusual for her when intensely interested in a subject, the young woman had gone through countless deliberations of her own devising. It was her mind versus itself, thinking of every possible objection and energetically considering all angles of an argument.

For some questions she could not find an answer that fully satisfied her. The young boy earlier that morning reminded her of her latest inquiry: why did the innocent suffer? For what purpose did this little boy's torment serve? He and his mother were poor, on top of it all!

She bit her lip at the many injustices she knew of, most of which she had never experienced in her own comfortable and altogether sheltered life. She knew some questions did not have answers, at least for now. Yet she had a deep conviction that Jesus was and would always be—what was the word the Elder used?—*unequaled*.

The young woman recalled how she had first met the elderly priest. One day finally fed up with the countless betrothal offers, more often than not from haughty noblemen, she announced to her mother that she would not marry anyone who did not think, act, and even look better than her.

"*Look* better than you?" her mother repeated, astonished at her daughter's demands.

"Yes!" the young woman pouted. "And he better be richer than me as well!"

Knowing her daughter's great kindness and beauty could only be surpassed by her well-admired (and often tenacious) intellect, the wise mother directed her to the Elder. "He can guide you on the topic of matrimony better than anyone else can," she had said.

Incredulously, the young woman went to see him. After one miraculous event after another, she eventually learned through the Elder not only who Christ was but how to love Him. Her mother, having secretly been a Christian all along, finally had her greatest prayer answered.

The young woman was convinced that God could *not* be another human's creation, like the idols she grew up worshipping. Had she not recently converted even the Emperor's wisest philosophers to Christ, when fifty of them were gathered to debate against her alone? Did not the Empress herself and hundreds of guards eventually confess Christ as God, with full knowledge that they would die for their new-found faith as a result?

A long sigh escaped her, one filled simultaneously with sorrow for the world's problems but also a strange contentment because *He* had overcome them.

"Why are you thinking so deeply, my dear Catherine?"

Catherine jumped at this, not having noticed anyone approaching.

"Mother!" The two women hugged each other tightly for several moments, one feeling she had finally gained her daughter and the other knowing she was soon losing not only her mother but everything she knew.

They walked quietly arm in arm, Catherine looking up at the sky pensively from time to time. She knew that Jesus suffered greatly and died, so that all suffering and death would be ultimately vanquished. Was she ready to die for Him?

Catherine answered her own question in the deepest recesses of her brave heart. She knew nothing could surpass choosing the King of Kings as her Bridegroom. Surely He was, and was immeasurably beyond, the most royal lover she could desire.

Catherine of Alexandria is considered by some to be a martyr from the early 4th century.[2] Before she became a Christian, the Elder told her he knew of Someone who could surpass Catherine in everything, exactly as she desired in a suitor. The Elder, speaking of Christ, told her, "His countenance is more radiant than the shining of the sun, and all of creation is governed by His wisdom. His riches are given to all the nations of the world, yet they never diminish. His compassion is unequaled."

---

2   Of note, Catherine's historicity is debated in some scholarly and religious circles. See Christine Walsh's work on Katherine of Alexandria.

Clouds

Looking broodingly at the darkening sky, the young man's frown deepened into a gloomy scowl. Thunder rumbled loudly, threatening the imminent rainstorm. In response, the large crowd hastened faster towards the gate finally coming into view. The mourning was palpable, with the loud wailing of women and relatives rising to the sky. *I hate rain. I detest it! Why is heaven sending rain on a day like today?*

It did not seem like the right time to think of anything except for the task at hand, but many responsibilities were weighing on this man's mind. Life seemed to be getting more merciless as time passed. Money, for one thing, was harder to come by after his father's death several years ago. Although some days it seemed as though they were barely surviving, his mother and sister, now in his care, seemed to always thank God still. He, on his part, was not inclined to be quite so grateful. And then his aunt's son—he furrowed his eyebrows as the thunder reverberated in the sky. He tried to think of a time when his cousin was not a part of his childhood memories, but Binyamin was present in all of them. After all, he was the favorite cousin, practically his brother.

The man could not move his right arm shouldering the weight, so he wiped his eyes with his left hand. The weather had been uncharitably arid for many weeks, and the long-awaited rain was finally about to arrive. Did it have to come *today*?

The group kept trudging forward, while the man tried in vain to locate his feet through vision blurred from emotion. He told himself to put one foot forward and then the other. Left, right. Left. Right. The air was still heavy with the promise of an impending downpour; but the rain, as if out of spite, did not fall.

Without effort the man's thoughts went to Binyamin again. He had been the kindest boy of the family, always ready to help anyone who asked him for a favor. Why had he especially cared for the vulnerable? He would have happily given his own loaf of bread to a beggar, even on a day like today! The man's sorrowful face faintly lit up at the remembrance of his cousin. Everyone who had known the boy could not help admiring his noble nature. Perhaps the death of Binyamin's own father had inclined his heart towards others, especially those who were forgotten by the elders.

The softness that Binyamin's memory brought to the man's coarse features disappeared as quickly as it came. His deep indignation, now a constantly returning companion, set his heart ablaze yet again. Where were the priests when the fatherless were going hungry? When the childless had neither clothes nor home? How could the religious leaders pray to God placidly from lavish homes while many of their own people were crying out to Him, with barely a roof over their heads?

And as though I did not have enough to contend with, the man thought bitterly, *I have just lost a man I considered my brother and will now take care of his grieving mother!* His mind struggled to remember the verse Binyamin would recite to him during the many trials they suffered together as children. The man knew that although this sweet boy was several years his junior, Binyamin seemed to possess greater trust in divine providence. The older cousin could picture the boy's eyes shining with expectation as he quietly repeated the Scripture: "For the LORD your God is God of gods and Lord of lords, the great God, mighty and awesome, who shows no partiality nor takes a bribe. He administers justice for the fatherless and the widow, and loves the stranger, giving him food and clothing."

Where was God now? Partiality and bribery, through the corrupt elite, seemed to focus their harm on the already brokenhearted. Rarely was justice executed, least of all for the orphan and widow!

At this point, the loud lamenting of the people intensified to a crescendo; the clouds of dust rose faster from their quickened shuffles; and the man's heart was relentlessly sinking into deeper grief—it was all too much to bear!

He thought he slightly buckled then, from not only the external weight he was carrying but also the internal agony dragging on his soul. Confound this Galilean dust! Was it soil or tears that were choking him?

But the other bearers had come to a sudden stop, and the man's attention was finally jolted to their furtive whispers.

"What did He say? Why did we stop?"

"He told her not to cry!"

"Who did?"

"The prophet from Nazareth—Jesus. He healed a centurion's servant not too long ago."

"Yes, close to death they say!"

"Why is He touching the bier?"

"Did He know Binyamin?"

The man silently repeated what he had just heard. *He told her not to cry.* Didn't all of Nain know that this poor woman was a widow and had just lost her only son? That she and the rest of his family may very well not afford a meal not long from now? *Execute justice for the orphan and the widow,* he now demanded silently from God with growing anger. *Execute justice for the widow!*

His indignation was rising quickly as he shifted his focus to the Man before him, of whom he knew very little. He looked both sorrowful and compassionate, as though He too was a relative of the boy that by all accounts had died at an incorrect time. The rain had started to quietly fall, and with it the dust slowly began to settle.

The man saw Jesus looking directly at Binyamin's body. He could not believe what he heard next.

"Young man, I say to you, arise!"

The words were spoken clearly, authoritatively. Jesus had said the words so firmly that the man and all those who heard Him could not help but secretly feel that Binyamin would indeed immediately rise. *What ridiculous, foolish hopes!* they each thought to themselves.

Then, a loud singular gasp of shock from all present went up as the rain began to fall harder, and Binyamin not only rose to a sitting position but began to immediately speak with them!

What ensued was a tumult of fearful shouts and joyful praises that saturated the wet air. Amidst the clamor, many embraced while others pressed their way through the crowd towards Jesus and Binyamin. All the while, the man was being pushed farther away from the two by the growing multitude. "A great prophet! Among us!" someone shouted. "God has visited his people!" yelled another.

Amidst the blurred chaos, the man was able to see Jesus guiding Binyamin to his mother. Her thin face was visibly full of mixed emotions. Grief had been etched there years ago, but at this moment she looked dazed, with a fresh set of tears in her eyes from joy rather than anguish. He watched the mother and son embrace as Jesus turned and walked away.

The greatest event in history has just occurred before my eyes! the man thought. Although a part of him wanted to run immediately to Binyamin, he was surprised to find that he had a much greater, burning desire to run after this Jesus. *If He could raise a dead man, surely He can answer a thousand questions about life and death and everything between them*, the man thought. The Scripture's words came back to his mind: *For the LORD your God is God of gods and Lord of lords, the great God, mighty and awesome.*

The LORD your God is God of gods and Lord of lords, the great God.

He is the great God.

The rain continued to fall, unwanted at that moment but needed. It had settled the dust into silence, and the man felt as though many of his own clouds of despair had similarly quieted down for the time being.

Perhaps he would meet Jesus again and speak with him. The man started to walk, then run, towards Binyamin. It was now his turn to share the Scripture's words, with a faith in them he had never quite known before.

Luke 7:11–17 recounts the incredible miracle of the raising of the dead son of the widow from Nain. Although the story here fictionalizes the name of the raised son and the details of his extended family, we do know that in first-century Palestine there was much corruption among the religious leaders. This left those who were already often vulnerable, such as widows and orphans, further neglected. The verses quoted are from Deuteronomy 10:17–18.

Chains

He quickly fingered the golden necklaces hanging heavily around his neck, a habit he formed many years ago when he was elated, nervous, or frustrated. At the present moment, he was a mixture of all three emotions: elated because of the evening plans, and equal parts nervous and frustrated because of further hindrances he soon expected. The man hurried into his estate and hastily trotted through the silent hallways. Trying to locate his wife, he passed through many well-furnished rooms, wondering yet again how the richly painted walls and mosaic-filled floors could emanate such coolness and vacuity.

"There you are—my dear!" The last two words were sputtered rather than spoken by her husband, and the short woman's already arched eyebrows shot up higher. Who could blame her? She had not heard an affectionate word for many years.

"Where have you been? What is going on?"

The rather stout man let out a merry laugh at her questions, and he hid his grin with hands covered in gold rings.

"My dear!" He repeated the two words, which tasted rather sweet now in his mouth, and cautiously put his arms out to hold his wife's shoulders. She was stunned at this attempt to be tender and too bewildered to ask how the husband who had left that morning was an entirely different person from the one before her.

"You remember earlier today I was going to the house near the large, old sycamore tree we used to meet at—the family with the two sick children, they live right there, everyone in Jericho knows them! Completely overdue on their tax collection! (But *do* you remember that sycamore tree, how much we loved it when we were younger?)—at any rate, imagine me running eagerly to see if they had scraped some money together, *anything*, and all of a sudden I hear several people talking to each other that *He* was coming by soon—"

"Who is *He*?" his wife asked incredulously, wrinkling her normally pouty nose.

"Why, Jesus from Nazareth! I told you many months ago I wanted to meet Him—not for money, just merely for my amusement; He has done miracles supposedly and that sort of thing—when today I realized here was my chance to see the Man! Not alone, of course, but with a large crowd, and—"

He paused his whirlwind of words and hesitated, unsure of how to relate what came next.

"Go on." The woman said this in her usual indifferent tone, but for her the two words were encouragement nonetheless. Her husband immediately perceived this and looked at her in turn with surprise. They were accustomed to speaking with each other neither intimately nor delicately.

"Well, you see—I have thought about Him often since hearing of Him. You see, He is not *any* ordinary Man. He cares for the *poor*." He stopped here, remembering his initial disgust at this. "He heals those who no one cares for—imagine touching *lepers*! He has said He can forgive sins." He looked at his wife to see if she was understanding. She nodded slightly, not sure of what to say but quietly telling him to continue.

The man took a deep breath in and sighed.

"I have been thinking—" He looked around and waved his arms to signal their house and the extravagance that had accumulated within it over many years. "I have been thinking how we have everything in the world, and yet—He talks about having *more*." The man took another deep breath in. "I think I have always known somewhere inside of me that—there is more than money, and riches, and that sort of thing." His voice trailed off at the end of his sentence. "And that is why, perhaps, sometimes—I have felt as though I do not have anything at all."

His face fell recounting this rather recent discovery, again reminded of its heavy weight.

"But then—" The man quickly raised his head to look at his wife, his face beaming with pleasure again. "I don't know what it was, dear, I really don't understand what happened next—perhaps it was the result of thinking for many months, and wondering how the devil things can change or if I could find the riches that Jesus spoke of—but the solution seemed to be in at least seeing Him, if I could not meet Him directly." Here he paused, and his face, which had not exuded real joy for many years, lit up with a laugh again.

"So then?"

"So I climbed it!"

"Climbed *what*?"

"I climbed that devil of a tree!"

The woman looked at her beaming husband astonished, not quite as amused as he. He continued.

"You know I would never be able to see above the crowd, the *tall* man that I am," Zacchaeus said with jovial sarcasm. "But I knew I *had* to see Him. And the best part is yet to come!" He rubbed his hands together with gleeful excitement.

"I saw Jesus approaching the tree, about to walk past—but He suddenly looks right up at me! *Me*! He saw me up there in our sycamore, can you imagine?" Zaccheaus laughed heartily and slapped his knee in amusement. His wife could not help a small smile at this absurd scenario.

"Jesus then says, 'Zacchaeus, hurry and come down, for I must stay at your house today.' He *must* stay at *our* house!"

With this the wealthy man, who felt rather poor in spiritual treasures at that very moment, stifled a loud sob. His wife, whose heart unknowingly had been changing since her husband had come home that afternoon, was surprised to feel tears come to her own eyes.

"What do we do now, Zacchaeus?" She hesitated, not knowing if she should say anything else. But after a few moments of silence, she finally decided to add in a cool manner, "He is welcome here." Such agreement with her husband was very unusual for her, and both knew it.

"He is here—well, not *here* in the house, just outside of it, I told Him I would like to speak with you before—" Here Zacchaeus stopped and hesitated again. "You know—people are always around Him, the townspeople and His followers and that sort of thing. And some grumbled—of course, some did not like hearing that He would come to *my* home." Here he paused, looking rather grim. "Sinner" did not have a very attractive ring to it when one was personally called by the word. "I heard the grumbling, and—you remember how I used to get fired up about things I cared for, and so—I told Him, 'Look, half of my possessions, Lord, I will give to the poor, and if I have defrauded anyone of anything, I will pay back four times as much!'" Zaccheaus tried to avoid his wife's gaze, fearful of her reaction to this impulsive pronouncement. Not hearing a response, he continued.

"This was only moments ago, right as we approached the door. Just now! And you know what He told me after? 'Today salvation has come to this house, because he, too—'" Zacchaeus faltered. Then he repeated Jesus' words in a quiet, trembling voice, "'Because he, too, is a son of Abraham.'"

Zaccheaus and his wife stood there silently for several moments, the words sinking deeply into the space around them. He then said something so softly that his wife could not hear it. "What did you say just now, Zacchaeus?"

"He cares for us, my dear. He cares for the poor, rich—all of us. I suppose—rather odd to think of it, but—I suppose any of us can be broken. 'For the Son of Man came to seek out and to save the lost'—that is what He said."

The two, who could not remember the last time they had a heartfelt conversation, embraced at that moment and held each other. In a rather short span of time, the estranged husband and wife felt as though invisible strings were rapidly connecting their hearts once more to each other and to something, or Someone, else. The couple was unsure of what would come next, but without any further verbal exchange, they *were* certain of two things: that they were having Jesus over for dinner and that they would follow through with Zacchaeus' promise.

Soon after, Zacchaeus' wife left the room to quickly fetch the servants and bring their distinguished guest in. Zacchaeus lingered a bit longer and touched the gold jewelry hanging on his chest. He slowly removed the chains, feeling unfettered for the first time in many years. He wouldn't be needing those anymore.

The story of Zacchaeus is found in Luke 19:1–10. Although details of his personal life, including his wife, are not mentioned in the gospel, Zacchaeus's meeting with Jesus completely changed him. The once corrupt tax collector is believed to have later become a bishop of Caesarea.

Green

With his eyes closed, the man took a deep breath in, savoring the familiar sea air. He breathed out slowly, trying to calm his troubled thoughts which from time to time gnawed at his happiness. Images of John's death came and went between thoughts of the miracles happening as of late—in fact, as recently as that very day. The man shook his head, momentarily freeing himself from memories that collided together and confused him.

He opened his eyes and looked out at the water. He remembered how, even as a young boy, in a boat with his father and brother, the colors of the sea would leave him breathless at certain times of the day. At this moment, as he had seen so many times before, the sun was coaxing the water to shimmer in hues of emerald and jade. After such an exhausting day, the sea invited but could not persuade him to swim in it. There was still much work to do.

He could hear the others nearby, talking excitedly with the Teacher and sharing stories from the day. His stomach growled noisily, urging him not to ignore it any longer. His was the most tired type of exhaustion, as though he had fished all day and night. He half-smiled to himself. *Well, I was fishing in some sense.*

The man turned around and took in the view. Here was a sea of green grass, with an increasingly greater number of people walking towards the Teacher. He sighed deeply. It would be a long evening.

Some time later, one of the disciples finally approached their Rabbi. He and the others had conferred that the day had been long spent.

"This is a deserted place, and already the hour is late." He waved absentmindedly towards the crowds, as though they were a bothersome swarm of flies. "Send the multitudes away, that they may go into the villages and buy themselves food."

The man who had been looking out at the sea instinctively knew this proposal would not satisfy Jesus. He was not surprised when the Teacher answered the disciple who had spoken, "They do not need to go away. You give them something to eat."

Someone audibly muttered to himself, loud enough for the others to hear, "Shall we go and buy two hundred denarii worth of bread and give them something to eat?" A few grumbled their strong dislike of this proposed solution.

As though He heard it all, Jesus focused his attention on a particular man, named Philip. "Where shall we buy bread, that these may eat?"

Philip, ready to underscore the impracticality of the situation, quickly responded with, "Two hundred denarii worth of bread is not sufficient for them, that every one of them may have a little!"

The man finally focused his gaze, which had drifted to the sea again, back to Jesus and the other disciples. *Couldn't He feed the multitudes?* the man silently asked. He had healed withered and paralyzed limbs, the mute and the blind. The dead were raised! And He had power not only over health and illness. Had not a storm on this very sea been stilled? The man remembered how Jesus had even boldly called Himself the Son of God—making Himself equal with God. Surely this was not impossible, then? It did not matter that such a feat would cost perhaps a year's wages. But where would they get such a large sum of money, and quickly enough at that?

The man suddenly caught sight of a young boy nearby with a basket. It looked as though it had some bread and fish. What if—no, that was quite impossible!

At that moment Andrew instinctively looked up to meet Jesus' gaze instead of contemplating the sea again. It was as though the Teacher was asking him to speak.

"How many loaves do you have? Go and see."

Did Jesus want to know how much bread the multitudes collectively had? Perhaps if everyone combined all the little food that they were carrying, then each person could leave with even a morsel or two. But what if—Andrew quickly thought about how, from healings to teachings to everyday occurrences, radical change was always possible. Every day a new discovery could be made, supernatural or otherwise. What if He had another plan entirely? With his Teacher, a miracle was never out of reach.

Andrew's heart beat faster as he looked at the boy's basket, then at Jesus again. "There is a boy here who has five barley loaves and two fish," he finally said. But as he verbalized his inner thoughts, a wave of embarrassment washed over him. The obvious impossibility of this solution made Andrew's faith waver. He quickly added, "But what are they among so many people?"

Having hoped to offer a solution but disappointed now at his inability to say or do anything useful, Andrew expected a similarly discouraged response from the Teacher. But instead, Jesus kept His eyes fixed on him. When He replied, "Bring them here to me," it was as though Jesus held onto Andrew's answer. It was as if He validated the reality spoken and what lay just beyond it. *Yes, the boy has five loaves and two fish. And they are plenty.*

As Andrew and the others collected the leftovers, his mind went over the details of the previous few hours. They had gathered the crowds into groups of fifty, and Jesus had indeed taken the little boy's loaves and fish. How incredibly small they looked as He looked up to heaven, blessed and broke them! How quickly did the disciples move as more, and more, and still more bread and fish needed to be passed out to the hungry masses!

How did they multiply? Andrew and the others could not explain it. Yet every single person they hurried past, whether man or woman or child, ate until they were completely satisfied. No one present could remember the last time when their bellies and hearts were full like this, beyond expectation.

Carrying a basket of fragments as Jesus had instructed them to collect, Andrew walked back to where the others were gathered. He counted them: one, two, three… was it possible? But of course, there would be twelve baskets of leftovers, not one more or less. Every one of Jesus' disciples was carrying his own individual confirmation of how God provided for each of them, for each of the thousands gathered there.

Andrew looked off into the distance and remembered the sea's blue-green brilliance from earlier in the day. He thought too about the hues in the grass and hills and sky, noting they were never miraculous in and of themselves.

Yet they were extraordinary. Creation could not help but glorify God's ineffable being. It was not only nature that moved Andrew. How often in the years before knowing Jesus had a conversation with a good friend, or a seemingly insignificant but kind deed, or an unreserved, hearty laugh been miraculous in its own right? Surely no demon was cast out nor blindness cured. Yet the beauty in those moments nudged his heart to something larger than life itself.

As he placed his basket next to the others, Andrew overheard a person saying to his companion, "This is indeed the prophet who is to come into the world." *Yes*, he thought quietly, *He is indeed the prophet, and much more.*

The incredible account of the feeding of the 5,000 is found in Matthew 14:13–21, Mark 6:30–44, Luke 9:10–17, and John 6:1–14. St. Andrew was one of the twelve close followers of Christ, and he, like his brother St. Peter, was called by Jesus as a fisherman. Both brothers would eventually be martyred by crucifixion.

Crowns

As Euphemia looked out from the balcony at the garden below, she could not help smiling at the pleasant scene in front of her. Her husband was hiding behind a shrub affecting an enemy soldier, while their young son was galloping on an imaginary horse. Peals of laughter were heard as Eudoxios jumped out from the brush, simultaneously surprising and hugging the gallant young knight. Euphemia laughed quietly and rang a bell to signal supper time.

Hours later, after they had eaten the warm meal and sang a few hymns all together, the young boy crawled into his mother's lap and asked her for a story.

"What story are you thinking of, my dear?" the pretty woman asked of her son.

"Mama, you know which one!" the little boy exclaimed.

So Euphemia began to say the parable. The young mother had recounted this particular story so many times that she could recite it word for word, while her thoughts were occupied by a completely different subject. Euphemia knew it was a bad habit, but she could not help ruminating now over her newest set of fears. Eudoxios had military summons again, and as always before he left, she was sleepless the preceding nights. As difficult as it was to admit to herself, she had recently been feeling somewhere deep inside her that soon her husband would not come back to them. Whenever this painful premonition surfaced, Euphemia would first pray fervently that it did not portend reality; then she would pray that Eudoxios would at least live long enough for the children to later remember him.

While simultaneously thinking thus and recounting the parable, Euphemia had been absentmindedly looking down at her son. But at that moment she suddenly focused her thoughts on the boy. His large brown eyes, framed by thick eyelashes, looked very serious as they concentrated on hers. *Those lovely features are from my side of the family*, Euphemia could not help thinking proudly to herself. While still talking, she cupped his square chin in her delicate hands and admired the curly crop of hair in front of her. *What a beautiful child inside and out—* and at that moment, like so many other times before, she fervently thanked God and the Virgin Mother in her innermost being.

Euphemia softly stroked her son's hair as she concluded the story. "And to—"

Here the young boy chimed in: "—everyone who has, more will be given." He quickly sat up and looked expectedly at his mother, grinning from ear to ear. Then Euphemia asked the question that always followed the parable. "So, my sweet boy, if the Lord gives you one mina, how many minas will you give back to Him?"

The young boy, with a triumphant smile, nearly shouted his response: "The whole mina!"

⁓

Several years later, Euphemia was writing a letter one evening when her son came home and deftly laid his lanky limbs out on the ground. Stretching his weary muscles, the young man greeted his mother, noting the gray hairs that had appeared since his father's passing. *She still looks pretty and youthful, but much more wrinkled!* he thought. *I'd better not tell her.*

Seeing her son distracted with a new parchment, Euphemia's mind went through a sequence of rapid-fire images as it often did when her son came home. The children and mothers in church. Weeping at home. Weeping in front of the Virgin's icon. Weeping and praying, and one day hearing the icon softly say, "Amen." Soon after, she was pregnant with this long-awaited child.

Mina now looked very much like his handsome father (God rest his soul!), but Euphemia was happiest thinking he had also inherited Eudoxios' gentle bravery and quiet resolve. *He has been strong for me and his sister*, she thought, *even though he has not yet reached his second decade!*

Despite their suffering, the children were visibly growing, and Euphemia was herself undergoing several invisible transformations. Although they noticed the change in their mother, Mina and his sister did not know how to acknowledge her intentionality with them. On her part, Euphemia could not help it, as she was often reminded of life's temporality. To the children, having their mother fully present with them made the topic of conversation or the task at hand much more meaningful. Euphemia did not realize that a particular thought often running through her mind was responsible for this: *who knows when I too will be called home?*

More subtly, she had also begun offering more to God in prayer. Sometimes this looked like a request, such as for patience with the often-rambling neighbor. Other times it was praise, during the mundane and otherwise dreary housework. Still other times prayer was simply accepting reality, like the wrinkles she had recently acknowledged. It was a deliberate, slow process of continual sharing with God. In her mind, she *knew* that nothing was too small or too big to give back to Him. Now she prayed that her heart would one day follow suit with this rational conviction.

"Ask me, Mother."

Euphemia turned around to Mina who still lay stretched out on the ground. "Ask you what, my son?"

Mina turned and focused his eyes intently on her. "The question after the parable."

Euphemia struggled for a few seconds to comprehend, then recognition provided a soft smile to her face.

"How many minas will you give back to the Lord? Ten? Five? One?"

The young man waited a few moments to respond. "The whole mina." He said it quietly and almost distractedly, as though he was pondering other matters.

Such beautiful crowns!

The matter was decided, of course. He could not deny what he had seen, and did not the heavenly voice say the crowns were his already?

But how would it happen? And when? *Oh, do not worry about tomorrow*, Mina chided himself. *Sufficient for the day is its own trouble!*

He walked farther across the sandy dunes towards the direction of the city. Images of tortured believers rose in his mind, although it had been some time since he had fled for this solitary life. The wilderness rather than erasing memories seemed to sharpen them. *But what was told to the Virgin? Do not be afraid,* he recited to himself. *You have found favor with God.*

He shielded his eyes from the harsh sun and looked at where his destination should have been appearing. All he could see were the never-ending hills of desert. *Christ too traversed unknown paths. He and the blessed Mother and Joseph, right here in our land....*

Mina kept walking, thinking over the vision. There were three crowns revealed to him—what did the voice say they were for? Celibacy, asceticism, and martyrdom. Yes, he had always desired chastity. Asceticism he had struggled with, here in the wilderness. And as for martyrdom—wasn't that the call of every Christian? He could not boast of what he had seen. He kept repeating in his mind, *We are unprofitable servants. We have done what was our duty to do.*

Far in the distance the tops of the city walls gradually came into view, as though a mirage. Mina squinted his eyes, and indeed here a few rooftops were visible, there the gates of the city. He briefly considered how his military service had not prepared him for this, a final battle of sorts. *But Father and Mother equipped me. Let it be to me according to Your word.*

Mina quickened his pace, the fervor inspired by the vision growing increasingly stronger within him. "How many minas will you give back to the Lord?" he said to himself in a low voice, as though his mother was present to ask him the question one final time.

The whole mina, he thought.
The whole Mina.
All of Mina.

⟡

St. Mina is one of the great Egyptian saints martyred in the early fourth century. Mina's birth was considered a miracle granted through St. Mary's intercession, and we know he lived for a time in the wilderness where he was shown a heavenly vision of crowns. We do not know if Mina knew the parable of minas recounted in Luke 19, but his love for God is like the meaning of his name: "steadfast."

Endings

Thia never did like it when a good book ended.

She closed the novel reluctantly and hugged her knees, letting out a squeal from equal parts exhaustion and accomplishment. Her eyes burned as she shut them tightly, and she ran the plot through her mind while rocking back and forth. *The author is a genius! He said on page one what would happen in that last chapter!*

She got up, slowly stretched her arms out, and yawned audibly. Her face fell as she realized she did not know what to read next. There was always an assumption in Thia's mind, at the end of any delicious book, that she had just finished the greatest and last surviving work of fiction. Fortunately for the most part, this devastation usually lasted only an hour or two until she discovered her next novel to devour. In her current limbo between joy (derived from the book she had just finished) and worry (that she may never replace it), Thia plopped herself on the large leather armchair. It squeaked as she did so, making her giggle and look around more comfortably at the small library. Her grandmother liked to sit here quietly in the evenings, undisturbed by Thia's often rambunctious conversation. The young girl had learned after several tiffs not to disturb the matriarch while she was reading on what seemed to be her untouchable throne.

What did Nana like about this chair, anyway? And the books here on the table—such plain covers! As much as Thia loved to read, she had never dared to touch her grandmother's literature. She thought one was a Bible, it looked so old and large! And the other was a much smaller book, although it too was worn and lengthy. Thia cautiously picked the latter up as if it were made of crystal. For a moment she hesitated to look inside, but then quickly thought to herself, *I have nothing better to do! I'll just endure the woman's wrath.*

She hurriedly thumbed through the stories at first, then went back to the preface. *These people are* real? She slowed her pace of reading, trying to fully absorb the words. Being the avid reader she was, Thia could already tell the storytelling was not as descriptive as she was used to. But her imagination began to supply details around what the writer had penned in the most straightforward terms.

It seemed like it was a book about, well, holy people. Thia's eyes grew large from time to time as she read about real-life princesses and brave warriors, sinners turned saints and everything in between. She was so engrossed in the stories, constructing in her mind all sorts of castles, sailing ships, and desert caves, that she had not noticed her grandmother enter the room. The elderly woman, worn down from years of troubles, stopped at the library's entrance and quietly remained unnoticed. She looked at the young girl who had been made an orphan far too young and sighed heavily, thinking of all the trials they had gone through together (and caused each other) for almost a decade.

The grandmother's stern eyes softened a bit as she saw Thia thus engrossed, completely oblivious of her observer. Nana had tried many times in the past to have Thia read more Scripture, or research a saint or two; but the avid young reader disdained her guardian's literary recommendations, preferring to consume every fantasy and sci-fi novel she could find. The elderly woman had finally decided some time ago that it was best not to fight nor pressure the young girl and had left her to read as she wished.

Thia, still not knowing Nana was in the room, turned to a short chapter that was ear-marked and well-known to its owner. The edges of this particular section, rather than being clean and white like the other chapters, were covered with careful cursive handwriting. Thia read a few notes, quickly realizing that Nana's personal thoughts covered all the once-empty spaces of this chapter.

"She's my favorite."

Startled, Thia slammed the book shut and looked up to find her grandmother a few feet away from her.

"Nana! You were spying on me!"

"Well, you were reading *my* book."

Thia hastily got up to give Nana her usual seat, but the old woman motioned for her to remain where she was and sat on a chair opposite. Thia reluctantly sat back down and waited for the scolding to be over.

But when her grandmother stayed silent, Thia's curiosity could not help but ask the obvious question. "Why is she your favorite?"

"Mary Magdalene? Well, we don't know much about her. But we do know Jesus healed her from many demons. And that she was one of Jesus' close followers. You know, helping in His ministry. Mary was with Him in His darkest hour, and even after the Cross, she couldn't help but go to His tomb. She always seemed to me like she could not be anywhere but with Jesus. She was so—so strong-willed." Nana had been looking at the books as she talked rather than at Thia. Here, however, she and Thia looked at each other, and it was not lost on them that they too shared this character trait.

"And—" Nana hesitated. She was not the type to talk, and she certainly was not used to having a pleasant conversation with her granddaughter. But they were talking about Mary Magdalene after all, and she could not stop there. "She reminds me that life is complicated. When she was at the tomb, can you imagine the mess her life must have seemed? Here they thought they had found the Messiah, and then

He died. *Now what?* she must have thought. But she still goes to the tomb. And soon after the resurrection, Jesus leaves—I mean, He ascends. Life may have seemed to stop, again. But the Holy Spirit comes. The church is born." Here Nana looked thoughtful as she carefully chose her words. "It was not an ending, or even a beginning, but a continuation."

The elderly woman paused again to take a deep breath in. "I like to think that she simply would not stop seeking the Truth, with a capital T. Her life was probably not easy, but she did not stop following Jesus. Strong-willed and dogged. That is why she is my favorite. Dogged, I tell you."

Here Thia broke out in a sheepish smile. Clearly this was a reference to an argument they had where Thia used the same words to describe Nana. The young girl held the book of saint stories out to her grandmother, but the elderly woman shook her head. "It's yours. Keep it."

Thia could not hide her surprise at this gesture of generosity, knowing how Nana held very few things, and fewer people, close to her. In fact, Thia had grown up thinking she was not one of them.

The young girl looked thoughtful for a moment, then looked at Nana who seemed pensive herself. "But how do you know about her?" Thia asked. "I don't remember her much in the Bible."

Seeing she had brought down her granddaughter's guard, Nana nodded. "Yes, you're right. All of this is what I have gathered from my reading and prayer. As you read history and theology and philosophy, you learn more and more. Things in Scripture you didn't understand before, or maybe simply didn't see before, come to light."

Nana looked at Thia, a beautiful miniature replica of her daughter long gone now. Her lips quivered slightly at the striking similarity between the two, and she felt astonished at not having noticed the strong resemblance until now.

"You know—" Nana looked away to stop the tugging on her heart and keep herself composed. "Your mother called you Alathia for a reason."

Thia looked at Nana, perceiving that they were crossing uncharted territory of vulnerability. "It means 'truth,' right?"

Nana replied, "Yes. Your mother was beautiful. Like you, you know. She was beautiful and stubborn and rebellious. But she always wanted to know the truth. She wanted you to always seek the truth, too. And that is how she named you."

There was a moment of silence with an unmistakable sense of sorrow hanging in the air. Nana then laughed quietly and added, "In fact, she saw on the Internet that *alatheia* meant 'truth' and *zettitis* meant 'seeker.' So she wanted to call you a combination of both words—something along the lines of *Alathettitis!*"

Both of them laughed at this. "But thankfully, your father intervened. He convinced her that with a name like that, it would be hard for you to introduce yourself to people. And that mattered to your mother, who was something of a socialite." Nana, looking at the floor, smiled a little at the memory. "So they settled on, well, truth."

Thia and Nana sat in their own spheres of quiet for a few minutes, each with different but altogether sweet recollections of the past. Thia was the first to break the silence.

"Truth seeker," she whispered, more to herself than anyone else. The name sounded like a title conferred to a heroine at the end of a great novel.

"Yes, truth seeker. I think that is what you are. You read so much, and so well, that I think you are looking for truth, or rather capital T Truth, in what you read."

Thia looked quizzically at her grandmother, so the latter continued. "I have learned a lot from reading *that* Book," and Nana pointed at her old Bible on the table. Thia nodded slightly but looked at her grandmother still with questioning eyes.

"I used to read Scripture as a book only telling me how I should live, and what good versus evil is. I think it does those things still. But perhaps more importantly—it's difficult to explain, but I read it as a story. An account of people, very much real and very human, who did terrible and wonderful things. And all the while, God is with them, even walks among them, and simply loves them. And He tries to show them over and over again, 'Here I am! I have life to offer you that is more exciting and adventurous than anything you could have written.' God's great story unfolds through them. And I think it *still* unfolds to this day."

With this lengthy speech, Nana sat back and looked straight ahead, as though she had entered a world that could not be intruded upon. The tables certainly seemed to have turned, with Thia the talkative adolescent simply desiring to hear more from her normally reticent grandmother.

Seeing Nana still quiet, Thia asked, "But what does that have to do with what I read?"

Nana quickly looked at Thia as though awakened from a dream and smiled. "Oh, yes. I like that you are asking questions. What I was trying to get at is—I have found you can see God in everything. When you seek what is good or beautiful, you seek God Himself. Truth is good and beautiful, and the Truth is God."

Nana looked ahead of her, as though she again was in her own world, and said to herself, "'To the pure all things are pure.'[3]" Chuckling to herself, she added, "And something I came across recently: 'There is nothing so secular that cannot be made sacred.'[4]"

---

3   Titus 1:15.
4   *Walking on Water* by Madeline L'Engle.

Thia stayed silent, almost uncomfortably, as she normally spoke every few minutes if not deep inside a book.

"So—we can seek Truth. We can seek God?"

"Yes. And He seeks *you*, and will always do so. And—it is difficult. Life is complicated, and I am still learning, although I am so old. But it is worth it, I think. The search will hopefully be worth it. The men and women in these books"—Nana here pointed first at the large text on the table and then at the smaller volume in Thia's hands—"have encouraged me with that."

As Nana sank into her chair, exhausted from the conversation, Thia wanted to laugh and cry at the same time. She felt the beauty of her grandmother's words, and at the same time it seemed very unfair that life could not simply be whole. Almost impulsively, she got up and ran to Nana and gave her the tightest hug she could squeeze. The elderly woman likewise embraced her granddaughter and did not let her go for several minutes.

The two did not know how long they sat there side by side afterwards, talking about deep matters and nonsensical issues. When dusk started to enter the room, they finally walked over to the kitchen together for supper.

Although not yet fourteen, Thia had already experienced deep sorrow, and deep joy, many times in the past. Today, the two seemed to strangely mingle together. But she was beginning to feel that the world needed more joy—in fact, had room for more joy—beyond anything else. *Oh, there are just too many emotions!* she thought. It was confusing, but maybe that was a good thing. Nana spoke, after all, of still seeking the Truth up until now.

Was it really an adventure? Was a destination guaranteed? There were many questions on Thia's mind, and she was not sure if there were answers to all of them. But perhaps the search *would* be worth it. Perhaps today, even right now, was the end of a chapter so Thia could turn to a new one.

Questions for Reflection

"Gold"

1. The miracle with the bleeding woman is a story of healing. In how many ways was she healed? How was Christ touching *and* seeing her significant?

2. Who are the outcasts in today's world? Have you ever felt rejected or like an outcast as she did?

3. Christ gave her hope when she had none at all. How can we know this same hope is offered to us? How can I offer it to others?

"Lavender"

1. The account of St. Photini (the Samaritan woman) is read several times in the Orthodox Church's liturgical year. Consider how a Samaritan woman talking to a Jewish Man (Jesus) was significant

back then. What would an analogous scenario today look like?

2. Very significantly, Photini met Jesus at a well, and she is also believed to have died in a well as a martyr. How can her thirst for love be understood in this context?

3. We have a multitude of ways in the 21st century to satisfy our need for deep connection. Why is it sometimes still difficult to fulfill this need?

"Royal"

1. Catherine of Alexandria saw Christ as the King He is, far greater than any other person or pursuit. What does it mean, practically, that God becomes our truest love?

2. Our modern lives vastly differ from Catherine's, but many attributes of the human condition do not change despite time and geography. To set something or someone on a pedestal is a timeless human act. Consider the following list and how each item may compete for your attention, and ultimately your heart: school, work, service, entertainment, a significant other, child(ren), parents and siblings, friends, myself, body image, accomplishments, acknowledgement/honors.

3. For those items that made your list in the last bullet, how can you give the top three their appropriate attention without pushing God aside?

"Clouds"

1. Like the cousin of the young man who died, everyone is carrying a burden. Sometimes it is obvious, and often it is not. Consider this for a moment, and how that may change the way you approach people from day to day.

2. Think about a burden you are carrying right now.

    a. Have you experienced Christ lightening this or any other load you have had, even though it may persist?

    b. Think about how the members of the Body of Christ can help you carry it. Are they?

3. The cousin almost loses hope that God is present to help the oppressed. Is it possible to approach God when we have similarly lost hope?

"Chains"

1. Zacchaeus placed unhealthy importance on material wealth. What high expectations, if any, have you placed on your material possessions? On bank accounts, retirement plans, investments (if you have them)?

2. We can sometimes feel chained down unwillingly by bad habits, addictions, or unhealthy relationships. Consider if there is something/someone in your life that weighs you down or even harms you. What is one thing you can do to limit its/their effect?

3. The New Testament alludes to spiritual treasures often. Can spiritual/heavenly treasure co-exist with material wealth? If so, how?

"Green"

1. St. Andrew seemed to know that God delights in giving us impossible joy, like when Christ used the young boy's small fish and loaves to feed thousands. Think about a few times in your life where you experienced very deep, very real joy.

2. Do "miracles" need to be supernatural? Can they simply point towards God's presence in our lives?

3. Consider writing 3-5 things daily for which you are thankful.

"Crowns"

1. Contemplate how Euphemia may have offered Mina to God from his birth, or even before then.

   a. Consider applying this concept of offering to God something or someone precious in your life.

   b. How could Mina's crowns (of chastity, asceticism, and martyrdom) apply to you, even if, for example, you are married, living in an urban area, and not persecuted in any visible way?

2. Being persistent in doing good is difficult work. Consider a role you fill and where you may not be thanked. Why is it important to continue to be steadfast?

3. To be fully present and intentional in our modern-day world seems impossible at times. Consider a relationship where you need to be more present and think of two ways you can implement change.

"Endings"

1. Like Thia and Nana, some relationships in our lives may be broken or frayed, even those we value most. Think of a relationship you wish were better.

   a. What are aspects of it that are out of your control? What aspects do you have control over?

   b. Consider remembering the above person in a brief daily prayer. Your heart (and theirs) may one day change as a result.

2. Nana believes that the Bible and her relationship with the saints have helped her on her life journey. In particular, she finds commonality with Mary Magdalene. Have you had a similar experience, or the opposite? Do you desire a change in this area of your life? If so, take a moment to pray about it.

3. Nana speaks of seeking the Truth. Contemplate on one of the following questions: What is/Who is the Truth? Is seeking the Truth a process or an end-goal? How do we know if we have "found" the Truth? (Like Nana, it is okay to answer with, "It's complicated.")

4. Notice that names are important in many of these stories: Photini, Mina, and the fictionalized names of Zahava and Thia. What is the story behind your name? Are names actually important—why or why not?

5. In the story, Thia is supposed to represent you and me. Think about the chapters of your life story you have cherished. Think about those that you are happy have ended. What kinds of chapters do you hope to see unfold in the future?

www.ingramcontent.com/pod-product-compliance
Lightning Source LLC
Chambersburg PA
CBHW021220020426
42331CB00003B/401